Building
the
Titanic

The Making of a Doomed Ship

by Sean McCollum

CONTENT CONSULTANT:

Captain Charles Weeks

Professor Emeritus in Marine Transportation

Maine Maritime Academy

CAPSTONE PRESS

a capstone imprint

Velocity Books are published by Capstone Press,
1710 Roe Crest Drive, North Mankato, Minnesota 56003
www.capstonepub.com

Library of Congress Cataloging-in-Publication Data
Cataloging-in-publication information is on file with the Library of Congress.
ISBN 978-1-4914-0419-5 (library binding)
ISBN 978-1-4914-0423-2 (eBook PDF)

Editorial Credits
Lauren Coss, editor; Craig Hinton, designer and production specialist

Photo Credits
Alamy: Pictorial Press Ltd, 6 (right); AP Images: Kirsty Wigglesworth, 39, Michelle McLoughlin, 23 (top), Pat Sullivan, 20 (top), Ralph White, 12 (bottom); Capstone, cover; Corbis: Ralph White, 18, Suzanne Plunkett/Reuters, 40–41; Dorling Kindersley: 13 (top), Hans Jenssen, 14–15 (bottom), John Woodcock, 16 (top); Getty Images: De Agostini Picture Library/De Agostini, 34–35, Popperfoto, 38; Library of Congress, 6 (left), 7 (top), 7 (bottom), 9 (top), 16 (bottom), 24, 44; Maritime Quest, 4–5, 8, 9 (bottom), 22, 25, 26, 28 (top), 28 (bottom), 29 (top), 29 (bottom), 30, 31 (top), 42, 45 (top); Newscom: Design Pics/Ken Welsh, 11 (bottom), Lefranc David/ABACA, 11 (top), Peter Muhly/AFP/Getty Images, 36, 37 (bottom), Ron Asadorian/Splash News, 37 (top), Splash News/Christie's, 23 (bottom), World History Archive, 31 (bottom); Red Line Editorial, 45 (bottom); Shutterstock Images: optimarc, 43 (background); SuperStock: Science and Society, 17, 32, Universal Images Group, 11 (center), 19 (top), 20 (bottom), 21, 33; Thinkstock: Dorling Kindersley, 5, 45 (middle), 12–13, VladyslavDanilin, 19 (bottom), Zoonar, 45 (ship icon); Weldon Owen: Leonello Calvetti, 10, 14–15 (top)

Artistic Effects
Shutterstock Images

Source Notes
P. 27 • from an interview with Helen Madden for the program *Up Country*, first broadcast January 8, 1976. www.bbc.co.uk/archive/titanic/5054.shtml; P. 31 • from "The Miracle," by Filson Young. Published in *The Titanic Reader*. Edited by John Wilson Foster. New York: Penguin Books, 1999

Printed in the United States of America in Stevens Point, Wisconsin.
032014   008092WZF14

Table of **Contents**

INTRODUCTION
The Launch of 401 4

CHAPTER 1
Dreaming Up Giants...............6

CHAPTER 2
Strength, Power,
and Luxury 12

CHAPTER 3
From Sketches to Steel.........24

CHAPTER 4
Style in Three Classes 34

CHAPTER 5
Final Preparations 42

GLOSSARY...............................46

READ MORE 47

CRITICAL THINKING
USING THE COMMON CORE 47

INTERNET SITES...........................47

INDEX..48

The Launch of 401

I n the shipyard, workers often referred to the ship by its build number: 401. But everyone knew its name: *Titanic*. The name fit. It was the largest ocean liner of its time.

For two years 401 grew in size. Day by day, piece by piece, workers added more and more parts to the ship.

On May 31, 1911, bands played as thousands of people flowed toward the shipyard. They had come to watch and celebrate 401's launch. Workmen received the order to stand clear. A red rocket tore into the sky. Then workers released the equipment holding 401 in place. The crowd cheered loudly as the ship slid into the water. A minute later RMS *Titanic* floated for the first time.

FACT: Along with passengers, ocean liners carried mail and cargo between the continents. *Titanic* and other British ships carried the title of RMS, short for "Royal Mail Steamer."

Titanic sank on April 15, 1912, after striking an iceberg in the North Atlantic Ocean.

The ship was not done yet. It would be nearly a year before the great ship was ready to depart on its maiden voyage. Altogether it took three years to build *Titanic*. But when disaster struck on the night of April 14, 1912, the giant ship sank in less than three hours.

Titanic launches in Harland and Wolff's Belfast shipyard in 1911.

CHAPTER 1

Dreaming Up Giants

WHITE STAR LINE.

"OLYMPIC."
45,000 TONS.
or
"TITANIC."
45,000 TONS.
THE LARGEST STEAMERS
IN THE WORLD.

To NEW YORK,
From SOUTHAMPTON—CHERBOURG—QUEENSTOWN.
From LIVERPOOL—QUEENSTOWN.
To BOSTON,

CUNARD LINE
NEW·YORK LIVERPOOL

Cunard Line and White Star Line competed for passengers. They boasted about the speed and luxury of their ships.

Today jets fly passengers across the Atlantic Ocean in a matter of hours. In 1900, however, the crossing took about five days aboard passenger ships.

In Great Britain two companies dominated the transatlantic passenger ship business: Cunard Line and White Star Line.

In 1906 Cunard added two huge, fancy, and fast ocean liners to its fleet: *Lusitania* and *Maurctania*. Officials at White Star Line felt the need to match or beat Cunard.

FACT: Passenger ships of *Titanic's* era competed to cross the North Atlantic in the fastest time. Ships setting a new speed record received an unofficial honor called the Blue Riband. In 1907 *Lusitania* earned the honor. It became the first passenger ship to make the crossing in less than five days.

6

LUSITANIA AT A GLANCE

- **COMPANY:** Cunard Line
- **MAIDEN VOYAGE:** September 1907
- **LENGTH:** 787 feet (240 meters)
- **CAPACITY:** 3,125 passengers and crew
- **TOP SPEED:** 27 knots (31 miles per hour)
- **FATE:** Sunk by a torpedo in 1915, near the beginning of World War I (1914–1918)

MAURETANIA AT A GLANCE

- **COMPANY:** Cunard Line
- **MAIDEN VOYAGE:** November 1907
- **LENGTH:** 790 feet (241 m)
- **CAPACITY:** 2,967 passengers and crew
- **TOP SPEED:** 27 knots (31 mph)
- **FATE:** Retired and scrapped in 1934

Visionaries

As legend has it, the idea for *Titanic* took shape on a summer evening in 1907. J. Bruce Ismay joined William James Pirrie for dinner at Pirrie's London mansion.

Ismay knew the business of ocean liners. Pirrie knew how to build them. Ismay was managing director of the White Star Line. Pirrie was a partner in Harland and Wolff, one of the biggest and best shipyards in the world.

Ismay and Pirrie came up with a plan to compete with Cunard. They would build three superliners: *Olympic*, *Titanic*, and *Britannic*. The ships would not be as fast as Cunard's. However, they would be the biggest and most luxurious.

TITANIC AT A GLANCE

- COMPANY: White Star Line
- MAIDEN VOYAGE: April 1912
- LENGTH: 883 feet (269 m)
- CAPACITY: 3,547 passengers and crew
- TOP SPEED: 24 knots (28 mph)
- FATE: Sunk in April 1912

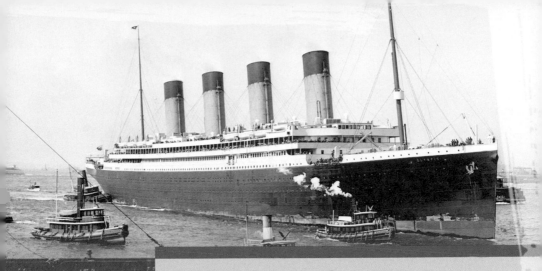

OLYMPIC AT A GLANCE

- COMPANY: White Star Line
- MAIDEN VOYAGE: June 1911
- LENGTH: 883 feet (269 m)
- CAPACITY: 3,547 passengers and crew
- TOP SPEED: 23 knots (26.5 mph)
- FATE: Retired in 1935

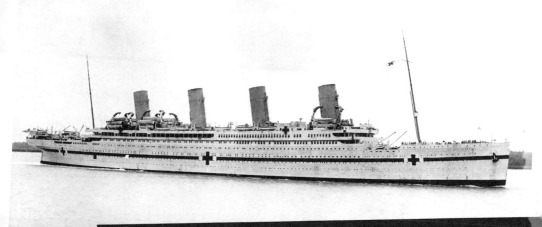

BRITANNIC AT A GLANCE

- COMPANY: White Star Line
- MAIDEN VOYAGE: November 1915
- LENGTH: 883 feet (269 m)
- CAPACITY: 3,547 passengers and crew
- TOP SPEED: 23 knots (26.5 mph)
- FATE: Never saw service as a passenger liner; became a hospital ship during World War I; sunk by an underwater mine in November 1916

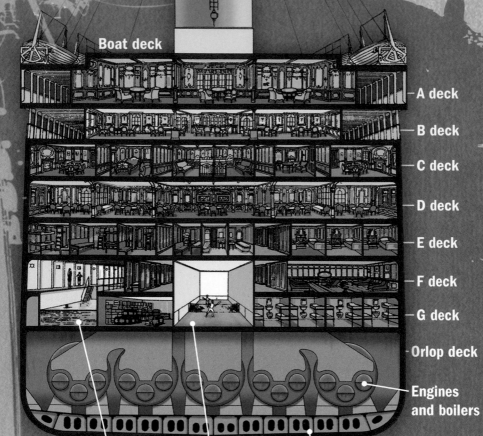

Boat deck

A deck
B deck
C deck
D deck
E deck
F deck
G deck
Orlop deck
Engines and boilers

Swimming pool   Squash court

Bilge (the bottom compartment of a ship that extends to a ship's sides)

White Star Line's Olympic-class ships would combine size and speed with the features of the world's fanciest hotels.

Designing Olympics

Pirrie and Ismay's vision began to take shape on paper in the second half of 1907. **Architects**, **engineers**, and interior decorators mapped out every inch of the first two Olympic-class ships: *Olympic* and *Titanic*. Their names fit their enormous sizes. Architects and draftsmen turned sketches and ideas into detailed drawings of the ships.

architect—a person who designs and draws plans for buildings, bridges, and other construction projects

Pirrie oversaw the technical plans—the basic structure and engines for the new ships.

WILLIAM JAMES PIRRIE

THOMAS ANDREWS

In July 1908 Harland and Wolff's designers presented the plans to Ismay and other White Star Line executives. Ismay approved the plans and signed the papers to begin construction.

Pirrie's nephew, Thomas Andrews, soon took over for Alexander Montgomery Carlisle as head of the design department for *Titanic*. Sketches became drawings, and teams of draftsmen turned those drawings into blueprints.

J. BRUCE ISMAY

engineer—someone trained to design and build machines, vehicles, bridges, roads, or other structures

CHAPTER 2

Strength, Power, and Luxury

As designed, *Titanic* was almost as long as three football fields. From the base of its **hull** to the top of its stacks, it was as tall as a 17-story building.

The ship's rounded stern allowed it to maneuver when docking.

A fourth funnel was added for looks and ventilation.

Central propeller

Side propeller

One central propeller and twin side propellers drove the ship.

The rudder steered the ship. *Titanic*'s rudder was about 78 feet (24 m) tall and 15 feet (5 m) wide.

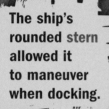

One of *Titanic*'s side propellers lies in the ship's wreckage on the ocean floor.

hull—the main body of a ship

The front three funnels were designed to release exhaust.

The crow's nest was a station for lookouts.

The wireless antenna was used for sending and receiving radioed telegraph messages.

The pointed bow could slice through open water.

The superstructure consisted of *Titanic*'s top three decks.

The bridge was *Titanic*'s command-and-control center.

stern—the back end of a ship

bow—the front end of a ship

When *Titanic* hit the iceberg, water flooded into six of the ship's 16 compartments.

Double-bottom hull

Hull and Bulkheads

The record sizes of *Olympic* and *Titanic* required new construction designs. The ships needed great strength to sail the North Atlantic's rough seas. Huge waves and fearsome storms could twist a ship to pieces.

Titanic's architects designed a double bottom for the ship. The double floor of steel reinforced the hull's overall strength. The open space between the two bottoms doubled as tanks for **ballast** and fresh drinking water.

Bulkhead

Bulkheads added to the hull's strength. These steel walls divided the lower decks into 16 compartments. If the ship collided with something, watertight steel doors in the bulkheads would quickly shut. Any leak would be contained in one compartment. Designers calculated the ship could remain afloat as long as no more than three compartments flooded.

ballast—any heavy material that adds weight to an object

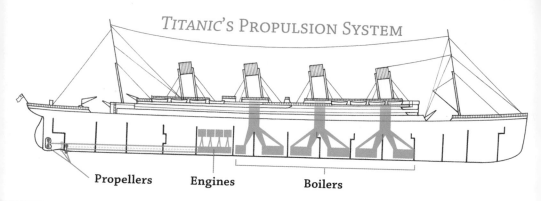

TITANIC'S PROPULSION SYSTEM

Propellers   Engines   Boilers

Power

Titanic's power came from the ship's huge engines. They powered the ship's three propellers.

Propellers

Long shafts transferred power from the engines to the propellers. The propellers moved the ship forward and backward. They also helped with the ship's turning ability.

The left and right propellers were 23.5 feet (7 m) in diameter. The central propeller was smaller, with a diameter of 17 feet (5 m).

Center propeller

Left propeller

Engines

    Titanic's design included three steam-powered engines. Two were piston engines that used a pumping motion. These were the largest ever built at the time. The engines drove the ship's **port** and **starboard** propellers. The third engine was a **turbine**. It used a spinning motion, similar to a fan. Exhaust steam from the other engines fed the turbine. It powered the central propeller.

Boilers are lined up and ready to be installed in *Olympic* and *Titanic*.

Boilers

    Titanic included 29 boilers heated by 159 coal-burning furnaces. The steam they generated powered the ship's three engines. The smoky, black exhaust poured through the ship's three forward stacks.

port—the left side of a ship looking forward

starboard—the right side of a ship looking forward

turbine—an engine powered by steam or gas; the steam or gas moves through the blades of a fanlike device and makes it turn

17

Command and Control

The bridge serves as a ship's central control center. From there, officers command the ship's speed and course. *Titanic's* main bridge looked down on the front deck. It contained the wheelhouse, where the steering wheel, known as the helm, was located.

This structure once held *Titanic's* steering wheel. It is all that is left of the ship's wheelhouse.

Titanic's officers would have ordered increases and decreases in the ship's speed using signal dials similar to this one.

For a vessel as big as Titanic, people needed a way to communicate between sections of the ship. Officers on the bridge and in the engine room had to signal to one another quickly and clearly. This was especially true in the event of an emergency.

Workers wired large signal dials between the bridge and the engine room. Using the dial officers could order a change in the ship's speed or direction.

Luxury

A palace sailing across the sea—that was the vision designers had for *Titanic*. The ship's second-class **accommodations** were better than first-class on other ocean liners. Even third-class cabins were tastefully crafted. White Star Line officials made it clear they wanted no expense spared on *Titanic*.

china from *Titanic* on the ocean floor near the wreck site

★ Designers selected plush furniture, crystal light fixtures, china dishware, and fine art.

★ Ship designs included two barbershops and a gymnasium with exercise machines.

★ Exotic Turkish baths provided a spa experience where first-class passengers could steam away their cares.

Titanic's reading and writing room provided an elegant space where first-class passengers could write telegrams or letters.

★ The sweeping Grand Staircase was set beneath a glass dome in the first-class areas. It showcased the ship's grand style.

★ Four elevators were also part of the design: three for first-class passengers and one for second-class.

★ Dining saloons, cafés, and lounges served passengers in several locations.

accommodation—a cabin fitted out for passengers

Safety

Experts at the time believed *Olympic* and *Titanic* were both practically unsinkable because of their design. Thick steel plating, a double bottom, and sturdy bulkheads gave these ships great strength. Engineers built other safety systems into the ships too.

Pumps

Titanic's designers gave the ship eight steam-powered pumps. These pumps could take in and pump out seawater. Five pumps balanced the ship. By adjusting water levels in the double bottom, the crew could make the ship ride more smoothly. Three bilge pumps pumped out wastewater as needed. Combined, these pumps could move 1,700 tons (1,542 metric tons) of water an hour.

Lifeboats

Titanic's layout allowed it to carry as many as 64 lifeboats. That was enough to rescue every passenger and crew member on a full ship. But regulations required a ship of *Titanic's* size to carry enough lifeboats for only about 960 people. In addition Ismay did not want lifeboats cluttering up *Titanic's* deck where passengers would stroll. When *Titanic* left on its first voyage, it carried 20 lifeboats, enough for 1,178 people.

After *Titanic's* sinking, the lifeboats were all that was left floating of the great ship.

Marconi Wireless

Titanic had its own Marconi room. This office housed a wireless telegraph. It was named for the inventor of that device. The wireless telegraph was new technology. It allowed ships at sea to send and receive messages and calls for help.

LIFE VESTS AND FREEZING WATER

Designers ordered more than 3,000 life vests for *Titanic*. However, these flotation devices offered no protection from the cold waters of the North Atlantic. In April water temperatures there can hover around freezing at 32 degrees Fahrenheit (0 degrees Celsius). Such cold water quickly drains heat from the body. People floating in it may pass out in less than 15 minutes. They are likely to die within 15 to 45 minutes.

a life vest from *Titanic*

CHAPTER 3

From Sketches to Steel

Harland and Wolff was considered the world's finest maker of large ships. Its shipyard in Belfast, Ireland, combined new and old technology. The latest steam-powered construction equipment did the heavy lifting. Horse-drawn wagons hauled materials as they had for hundreds of years.

Slipways

Workers built the hulls of *Olympic* and *Titanic* on slipways. A slipway is a large, sloped work area. To build *Olympic* and *Titanic* at the same time, the shipyard remade three large slipways into two huge ones. Workers reinforced the slipways with more than 4 feet (1 m) of concrete. There, the giant ships would rise and take shape.

When a hull was ready for launch, workers greased the slipway. Then gravity would pull the hull down the slipway and into the River Lagan.

The shipyard upgraded its facilities to build *Titanic* (left) and *Olympic* (right) side by side.

Arrol Gantry

A giant steel frame called the Arrol Gantry surrounded the ships. It supported huge cranes and other machinery that would be used in construction. Named for its designer, William Arrol, the frame also served as a work platform. Workers could use the gantry to access different parts of the ships as they were built from the ground up.

Cranes

On the gantry itself, workers could shift 16 moveable cranes to where they were needed. A huge central crane could lift 200 tons (181 metric tons) almost 150 feet (46 m) off the ground.

FACT: The River Lagan was dug out to be 32 feet (10 m) deeper. Otherwise the massive ships might hit bottom once they left the shipyard and steamed out to sea.

The Workers

Of the more than 15,000 workers employed at Harland and Wolff, about 3,000 worked on *Titanic*. Many jobs were dangerous. There was little for safety equipment or rules. During three years of construction, eight workers were killed and 28 severely hurt.

The men of Belfast took great pride in working on the massive ship. Most skilled workers, such as electricians, carpenters, and riveters, learned their trade as teenage apprentices. Skilled workers earned approximately £2 a week—about $250 in today's money. Unskilled laborers—those without special training—earned half that amount.

Workmen install *Titanic's* propeller shaft. Most of the workmen who built *Titanic* worked about 50 hours a week, performing muscle-burning physical labor.

apprentice—someone who learns a trade by working with a skilled person

Construction Jobs on the *Titanic*

JOB	RESPONSIBILITIES
CARPENTERS/ JOINERS	These shipyard woodworkers crafted fine furniture, cabinets, railings, and other wooden details for the ship's interior.
CAULKERS	These workers were responsible for making the ship's steel plating watertight.
DOCK WORKERS	These unskilled workers moved supplies and did other jobs around the construction site.
ELECTRICIANS	These skilled tradesmen installed more than 200 miles (322 kilometers) of electrical wire inside the ship. Electricity ran through this wiring to power *Titanic*'s lights and other electrical equipment.
FITTERS	These machinists prepared and modified metal parts for installation.
MOULDERS	As skilled steelworkers, moulders were responsible for customizing the hull plating.
RIVETING TEAMS	These teams were responsible for driving fasteners, called rivets, into the ship's steel plating.

“ If you had seen or known the process of extra work that went into the ship, you'd say it was impossible to sink her. ... It was a marvelous bit of work. ”

—*Jim Thompson, caulker on* Titanic

FACT: Workers used more than 3 million steel and iron rivets to bolt *Titanic*'s hull together. The rivets alone weighed about 1,200 tons (1,089 metric tons).

The Hull

Before the end of 1908, workers laid down *Olympic's* **keel**. Plans on paper began to turn into iron and steel. Soon the neighboring slipway and gantry were ready. The work crews were hired. *Titanic's* construction could begin.

The first task was building *Titanic's* hull. The hull was built in several overlapping stages that took more than two years to complete.

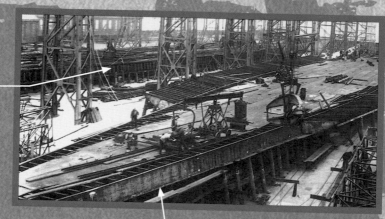

Titanic's keel

Olympic's **double-bottom hull**

Stage 1: Laying the Keel

Workmen laid down the *Titanic's* keel on March 31, 1909. From there, the ship's double bottom took form.

Stage 2: Framing

Steel beams rose from the ship's lower hull like a giant rib cage.

keel—the bottom of a ship

Titanic being plated

Stage 3: Plating

Olympic's plating complete

Workers riveted steel plates up to 1.5 inches (4 centimeters) thick to the frame.

Stage 4: Inner Framing

Inside the ship, workmen installed steel beams to support *Titanic*'s decks.

Titanic's C deck

Titanic's D deck

On May 31, 1911, the 883-foot (269-m) hull slid from its birthplace into the River Lagan. From there, tugboats towed it to the fitting-out basin where construction continued.

FACT: More than 90 years later, scientists tested rivets and plating raised from the wreck of *Titanic*. Some experts now suspect low-quality iron used in the rivets may have contributed to the ship's sinking.

Fitting Out

The shipyard's fitting-out basin was a man-made lake. It was constructed on the banks of the River Lagan. Crews installed the inner mechanical workings, decking, and interiors.

The work progressed from bottom to top:

Stage 1

A crane carefully lowered each of the 29 boilers to the lowest deck. Workers assembled the engines onboard.

Deck cranes help with heavy lifting on *Olympic*.

Stage 2

Deck laying began once the boilers and engines were in place. The plumbing, electrical, and mechanical work started as well.

Stage 3

Workers constructed the lounges, dining rooms, and passenger **berths**. They installed equipment in the kitchens and other service areas.

berth—a shelflike bed or bunk used as sleeping quarters on a boat or a train

Titanic's three exhaust-releasing funnels were placed on the ship before the fourth ventilation funnel.

Stage 5

On February 3, 1912, *Titanic* was towed to a dry dock. Unlike the fitting-out basin, the dry dock could be emptied. Once workers secured the ship, they pumped out the water. Workers installed the propeller shafts and propellers. Work crews applied coats of paint to the ship's exterior.

The dry dock gave workmen access to *Titanic*'s underside.

66 **The skeleton within the scaffolding began to take shape, at the sight of which men held their breaths. It was the shape of a ship, a ship so monstrous and unthinkable that it towered there over the buildings and dwarfed the very mountains by the water.** 99

—Filson Young, Irish journalist

Final Touches

With *Titanic*'s departure approaching, decorators picked up the pace of their work inside the ship. Designers wanted to impress passengers with convenience, comfort, and luxury.

Expert craftsmen built and installed cabinets and fireplaces. They added wallpaper and paneled cabin walls with fine wood. They laid down and polished wood floors. They put in carpet and tile. Plasterers and painters readied the ship's lounges, dining rooms, and hundreds of passenger cabins.

Titanic's Unique Features

★ electric heaters in some passenger cabins

★ a system of 50 telephone lines for passengers to make on-ship calls

★ running water in cabins, which was still rare in many homes at the time

★ a saltwater swimming pool

★ a clinic, including an operating room

★ a squash court

An illustration shows *Olympic*'s squash court, which was the same as *Titanic*'s. Squash is a British game played with rackets.

FACT: About 10,000 lightbulbs lit *Titanic*. Every cabin had electric lights. This was a rare convenience during *Titanic*'s time.

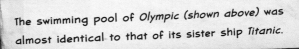

The swimming pool of *Olympic* (shown above) was almost identical to that of its sister ship *Titanic*.

CHAPTER 4

Style in Three Classes

In 1912 social classes separated most British neighborhoods and businesses. It was uncommon for rich and poor people to socialize with one another. Modes of transportation were segregated as well. *Titanic* was no exception.

Titanic's layout was designed with this class system in mind. There were separate dining rooms, cabin areas, and spaces on the top deck for the three classes of passengers.

Third Class

Most third-class cabins and common areas were located near the stern. Some cabins housed families. Single women shared group cabins near the stern. Single men shared group cabins in the bow.

Second Class

Cabins for second-class passengers were near the stern of the ship, ahead of the third-class passengers.

FACT: Each class on *Titanic* had its own style of dinnerware. Copies of the stylish first-class china are now sold as collector's items.

First Class

First-class accommodations were located on the upper decks. These included lounges, cabins, and suites. Suites were large cabins with their own bedrooms and bathrooms.

Crew

Crew members shared quarters in the bow. Officers' cabins were located on the upper decks. The captain and first officer's cabins were next to the ship's bridge.

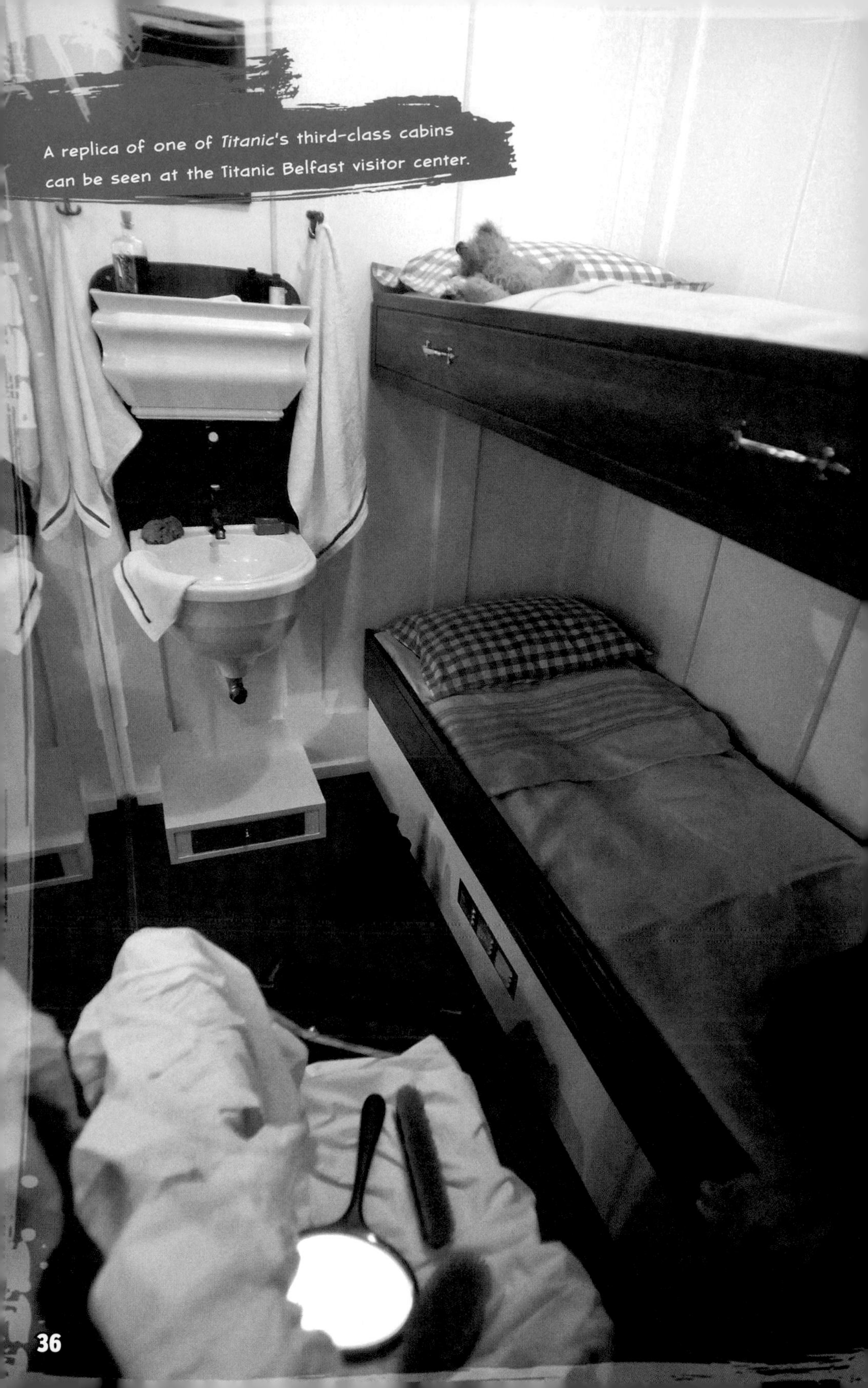

A replica of one of *Titanic*'s third-class cabins can be seen at the Titanic Belfast visitor center.

Third Class

Attracting third-class passengers was an important part of White Star Line's business. Most of these travelers were **emigrating** to the United States or Canada in hope of starting new lives. The company hoped third-class passengers would write to family and friends about their great experience on the ship.

A teacup from *Titanic*'s third-class dining room was recovered from the wreckage.

Titanic contained 220 third-class cabins. The rooms were snug but well crafted. They were often nicer than the homes many third-class travelers were leaving.

a third-class porthole recovered from the *Titanic* wreck

LIFE IN THIRD CLASS

- Some third-class cabins had two or four berths in the form of bunk beds.
- Dormitory-style cabins had six or 10 berths.
- Cabins near the stern included washbasins with cold running water.
- Passengers shared washrooms down the hallway from the cabins.
- Unlike on other passenger ships, crews on *Titanic* served meals in third class. Its third-class dining area seated up to 473 people at a time.
- Passengers could relax in a smoking room and lounge.

emigrate—to leave one's own country to live in another one

Second-class passengers who wanted to enjoy the ocean air could take a walk on their private promenade.

Second Class

Titanic's second class was equal to or better than first class on other ocean liners. White Star Line hoped to fill its 207 second-class cabins with middle-class travelers, such as businessmen, professors, clergy, and other professionals.

Second-class cabins were larger and more comfortable than third-class cabins. Furniture was crafted from mahogany, a beautiful dark wood. Each room had a cold-water washbasin, but all second-class passengers had to share bathrooms.

SECOND-CLASS PERKS

- Second-class passengers could relax in a lounge that doubled as a library. Passengers could perch on sofas or play cards or other games at square-topped tables. Cabinets held shelves of books for borrowing.

- Passengers wanting a breath of fresh air could stroll down the private second-class promenade.

- Men could smoke and relax in the second-class smoking room, in which women were not allowed.

- Men could pay to have a daily shave in the barbershop.

- Food for second-class passengers was prepared in the same kitchen as meals for first class. Crew members served meals in the second-class dining room.

A reproduction of one of *Titanic's* second-class cabins shows two beds that can be enclosed by curtains.

promenade—a deck on a ship where passengers can stroll

A replica of one of *Titanic*'s first-class cabins shows how comfortable and luxurious they were.

Electric lights

Wallpaper ⟶

Carpet

First Class

Titanic's first-class accommodations were designed to appeal to the richest of the rich. The unmatched luxury drew several of the world's wealthiest businessmen to sign on for the maiden voyage.

The first-class dining room was the largest room on the ship. With lush carpet and the Grand Staircase, it seated more than 500 people. First-class passengers could eat and drink as if dining at a fine restaurant.

FACT: American J. P. Morgan owned White Star Line. In 1912 he was one of the wealthiest men in the world. Morgan was scheduled to sail on *Titanic*'s first voyage but had to cancel at the last minute.

Interconnecting doors

Fine china

FIRST-CLASS CABINS

- First-class cabins had the finest furnishings and decorations on the ship.

- Guests could unlock interconnecting doors to turn neighboring cabins into grand suites.

- Some first-class cabins were equipped with telephones to make on-ship calls.

- First-class suites had private bathrooms with hot and cold running water.

CHAPTER 5

Final Preparations

Sea Trials

In the early morning hours of April 2, 1912, smoke rose from *Titanic*'s funnels. Down below, crews fired up the boilers. The coal-burning furnaces turned water into steam, creating power for the engines.

The ship was about to undergo sea trials. Officials conducted these tests to make sure *Titanic* was ready to carry passengers to sea.

Titanic passed every test easily. Officials signed the papers, giving the ship permission to sail. Shortly after 8:00 p.m. on April 2, *Titanic* left Belfast for the last time.

At about 6:00 a.m., on April 2, 1912, tugboats arrived to tow *Titanic* to the Irish Sea, where its sea trials would take place.

Titanic Sea Trials Checklist

☑ Measure a top speed of 20 knots (23 mph), and time how long it takes for the ship to drift to a stop.

☑ Stop and restart the engines at sea.

☑ Turn using just the rudder; then turn again using the port and starboard propellers.

☑ Turn in a complete circle at high speed.

☑ Execute an emergency stop by putting the propellers in reverse.

☑ Measure a cruising speed of 18 knots (21 mph) for two hours.

☑ Drop the ship's anchors.

FACT: *Titanic's* anchors weighed 15 tons (14 metric tons) each. It took 20 horses to pull a wagon carrying just one anchor to the shipyard.

Departure

On the morning of April 10, 1912, Captain Edward Smith's officers reported that *Titanic* was ready to sail. Its cargo was stowed, and the crew was onboard. *Titanic's* first passengers began arriving by mid-morning. The crew guided each class aboard through its own entrance.

On April 11 the White Star Line's newest, most magnificent ship left Queenstown, Ireland, for New York. Onboard were approximately 2,200 passengers and crew. They were sailing toward an unimaginable fate. Only 712 would survive the journey. Just four days later, the ship would sink to the bottom of the North Atlantic after striking an iceberg. More than 1,500 passengers and crew members died in the tragedy.

A newspaper headline tells the world of *Titanic's* sinking. Later the number of women and children saved was found to be much lower than first reported.

Titanic's Timeline

MARCH 1909–MARCH 1912
BELFAST, IRELAND: *Titanic* is built by Harland and Wolff in its shipyard.

APRIL 2, 1912
IRISH SEA: *Titanic* undergoes sea trials and passes. The ship sails to Southampton.

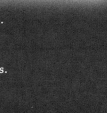

APRIL 10, 1912
SOUTHAMPTON, ENGLAND: *Titanic* picks up its first passengers and sets sail.

APRIL 10, 1912
CHERBOURG, FRANCE: *Titanic* picks up additional passengers.

APRIL 11, 1912
QUEENSTOWN, IRELAND: *Titanic* picks up its final passengers.

APRIL 15, 1912
NORTH ATLANTIC OCEAN: *Titanic* sinks after striking an iceberg.

APRIL 17, 1912
NEW YORK: *Titanic* is scheduled to arrive.

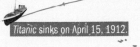

Belfast

Irish Sea

Queenstown

Southampton

Cherbourg

New York

Titanic sinks on April 15, 1912.

Atlantic Ocean

Glossary

accommodation (uh-kah-muh-DAY-shuhn)—a cabin fitted out for passengers

apprentice (uh-PREN-tiss)—someone who learns a trade by working with a skilled person

architect (AR-ki-tekt)—a person who designs and draws plans for buildings, bridges, and other construction projects

ballast (BA-luhst)—any heavy material that adds weight to an object

berth (BUHRTH)—a shelflike bed or bunk used as sleeping quarters on a boat or a train

bow (BAU)—the front end of a ship

emigrate (E-muh-grayt)—to leave one's own country to live in another one

engineer (en-juh-NEER)—someone trained to design and build machines, vehicles, bridges, roads, or other structures

hull (HUHL)—the main body of a ship

keel (KEEL)—the bottom of a ship

port (PORT)—the left side of a ship looking forward

promenade (prah-muh-NADE)—a deck on a ship where passengers can stroll

starboard (STAHR-burd)—the right side of a ship looking forward

stern (STERN)—the back end of a ship

turbine (TUR-bine)—an engine powered by steam or gas; the steam or gas moves through the blades of a fanlike device and makes it turn

Read More

Hopkinson, Deborah. *Titanic: Voices from the Disaster*. New York: Scholastic Press, 2012.

Stewart, Melissa. *Titanic*. National Geographic Readers. Washington, D.C.: National Geographic, 2012.

Wilkinson, Philip. *Titanic: Disaster at Sea*. Mankato, Minn.: Capstone Press, 2012.

Critical Thinking Using the Common Core

1. White Star Line hoped to compete with Cunard Line when it built its Olympic-class ships. What features did designers add to *Titanic* to attract passengers? (Key Ideas and Details)

2. How does the diagram on pages 12 and 13 help you understand *Titanic*'s key features and how they worked? If you were the ship's designer, would you have changed anything? (Craft and Structure)

3. Pages 22 and 23 discuss *Titanic*'s safety features. Why did so many people die in the sinking despite these safety features? What changes could have been made that would have allowed more people to survive? (Integration of Knowledge and Ideas)

Internet Sites

FactHound offers a safe, fun way to find Internet sites related to this book. All of the sites on FactHound have been researched by our staff.

Here's all you do:

Visit *www.facthound.com*

Type in this code: 9781491404195

Index

anchors, 43

Andrews, Thomas, 11

architects, 10, 14

Arrol Gantry, 25, 28

Arrol, William, 25

ballast, 14

Belfast, Ireland, 24, 26, 42, 45

berths, 30, 37

Blue Riband, the, 6

boilers, 17, 30, 42

bridge, 13, 18, 19, 35

Britannic, 8, 9

bulkheads, 15, 22

cabins, 20, 32, 33, 34, 35, 37, 38, 41

command, 13, 18–19

cranes, 25, 30

crew members, 7, 8, 9, 22, 35, 37, 38, 42, 44

Cunard Line, 6, 7, 8

decorators, 10, 32

departure, 32, 44

design, 10, 11, 12–13, 14, 17, 20, 21, 22, 34, 40

designers, 11, 15, 20, 22, 23, 32

dry dock, 31

emergencies, 19, 43

engineers, 10, 22

engines, 11, 16–17, 19, 30, 42, 43

first class, 20, 21, 35, 38, 40–41

fitting out, 29, 30–31

funnels, 12, 13, 31, 42

Grand Staircase, 21, 40

Harland and Wolff, 8, 11, 24, 26, 45

hull, 12, 14–15, 22, 24, 27, 28–29

icebergs, 44, 45

iron, 27, 28, 29

Ismay, J. Bruce, 8, 10, 11, 22

launch, 4, 24

lifeboats, 22

Lusitania, 6, 7

luxury, 8, 20–21, 32, 40

Marconi room, 23

Mauretania, 6, 7

Morgan, J. P., 41

officers, 18–19, 35, 44

Olympic, 8, 9, 10, 14, 22, 24, 28

passengers, 4, 6, 7, 8, 9, 20, 21, 22, 30, 32, 34, 37, 38, 40, 42, 44, 45

Pirrie, William James, 8, 10, 11

power, 16–17, 22, 24, 27, 42

propellers, 12, 16, 17, 31, 43

pumps, 22

River Lagan, 24, 25, 29, 30

rivets, 26, 27, 29

rudder, 12, 43

safety, 22, 26

sea trials, 42, 43, 45

second class, 20, 21, 34, 38

signal dials, 19

sinking, 5, 27, 29, 44, 45

slipways, 24, 28

speed, 6, 7, 8, 9, 18, 19, 43

steel, 14–15, 22, 25, 27, 28–29

telegraph, 13, 23

third class, 20, 34, 37, 38

wheelhouse, 18

White Star Line, 6, 8, 9, 11, 20, 37, 38, 41, 44